A Gift of Friendship

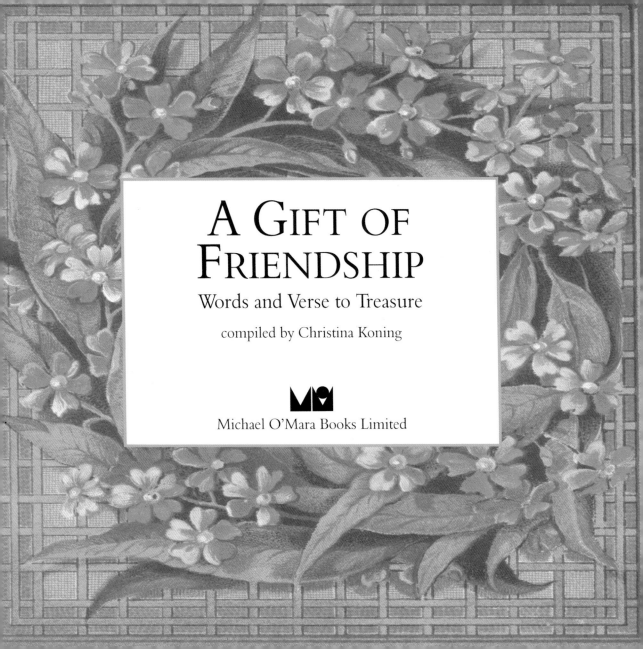

A GIFT OF FRIENDSHIP

Words and Verse to Treasure

compiled by Christina Koning

Michael O'Mara Books Limited

First published in Great Britain in 1999
by Michael O'Mara Books Limited
9 Lion Yard
Tremadoc Road
London SW4 7NQ

A CIP catalogue record for this book is available from the
British Library

ISBN 1-85479-335-7

1 3 5 7 9 10 8 6 4 2

Designed by Mick Keates
Formatted by Concise Artisans
Printed in Great Britain by Butler & Tanner Limited

Cover design: Slatter-Anderson

ACKNOWLEDGEMENTS

The publisher has to the best of its endeavours attempted to trace all copyright holders and wherever possible permission to use material has been sought and granted.

The publisher would like to thank the following for granting permission to reproduce copyright material: the four lines from 'Dedicatory Ode' reprinted by permission of The Peters Fraser and Dunlop Group Limited on behalf of: The Estate of Hilaire Belloc (p. 6); HarperCollins Publishers Ltd for permission to quote from *The Four Loves*: *Friendship* by C. S. Lewis (p. 6); The Estate of the Late Elizabeth Taylor and A. M. Heath & Co. Ltd for the extract taken from *The Rose, The Mauve, The White* – Copyright © Elizabeth Taylor 1958 (p.14); 'Buttercup Days' from *Now We Are Six* by A. A. Milne reprinted by permission of Methuen Children's Books (a division of Egmont Children's Books Limited) (p. 17); A. P. Watt Ltd on behalf of Michael Yeats for the extract from 'The Municipal Gallery Revisited' taken from *The Collected Poems of W. B. Yeats* (p. 41); The Society of Authors as the Literary Representative of the Estate of A. E. Housman for the extract from *A Shropshire Lad* (p. 45).

From quiet homes and first beginning,
Out to the undiscovered ends,
There's nothing worth the wear of winning,
But laughter and the love of friends.

HILAIRE BELLOC – FROM 'DEDICATORY ODE'

Friendship is unnecessary, like philosophy, like art... It has no survival
value; rather it is one of those things that give value to survival.

C. S. LEWIS – FROM 'THE FOUR LOVES: FRIENDSHIP'

Books and friends should be few but good.

PROVERB

A faithful friend is a strong defence; and he that hath found such an one hath found a treasure.

Nothing doth countervail a faithful friend, and his excellency is invaluable.

A faithful friend is the medicine of life...

Forsake not an old friend; for the new is not comparable to him; a new friend is as new wine; when it is old, thou shalt drink it with pleasure.

ECCLESIASTICUS 6:16

People will, in a great degree, and not without reason, form their opinion of you, upon that which they have of your friends... you are whatever the company you keep is.

LORD CHESTERFIELD

'It is of no use saying anything to you, Mary. You always take Fred's part.'

'Why should I not take his part?' said Mary, lighting up. 'He would take mine. He is the only person who takes the least trouble to oblige me.'

'You make me feel very uncomfortable, Mary,' said Rosamond, with her gravest mildness; 'I would not tell mamma for the world.'

'What would you not tell her?' said Mary, angrily.

'Pray do not go into a rage, Mary,' said Rosamond, mildly as ever.

'If your mamma is afraid that Fred will make me an offer, tell her I would not marry him if he asked me. But he is not going to do so, that I am aware. He certainly never has asked me.'

'Mary, you are always so violent.'

'And you are always so exasperating.'

'I? What can you blame me for?'

'Oh, blameless people are always the most exasperating. There is the bell – I think we must go down.'

'I did not mean to quarrel,' said Rosamond, putting on her hat.

'Quarrel? Nonsense; we have not quarrelled. If one is not to get into a rage sometimes, what is the good of being friends?'

GEORGE ELIOT – FROM 'MIDDLEMARCH'

My friend, my companion, held most dear,
My soul, my other self, my inward friend.

MARY SIDNEY HERBERT

True friendship is never serene.

MADAME DE SÉVIGNÉ

Friendship is to be purchased only by friendship.

THOMAS WILSON

In thee my soul shall own combined
The sister and the friend...

CATHERINE KILLIGREW

You meet your friend, your face brightens – you have struck gold.

PATRICE DIEHL

Surely we ought to prize those friends on whose principles and opinions we may constantly rely – of whom we may say in all emergencies, 'I know what they would think'.

HANNAH FARNHAM LEE

Fate chooses your relations, you choose your friends.

JACQUES DELILLE

Life is to be fortified by many friendships. To love and to be loved, is the greatest happiness of existence.

SYDNEY SMITH

In thought and sympathy we were one, and in the division of labour we exactly complemented each other. In writing we did better work together than either could do alone. While she is slow and analytical in composition, I am rapid and synthetic. I am the better writer, she the better critic. She supplied the facts and statistics, I the philosophy and rhetoric, and, together, we have made arguments which have stood unshaken through the storm of long years.... So closely interwoven have been our lives, our purposes and experiences, that, separated, we have a feeling of incompleteness – united, such strength of self-assertion that no ordinary obstacles, difficulties or dangers ever appear to us insurmountable.

ELIZABETH CADY STANTON – OF HER
FRIENDSHIP WITH FELLOW WRITER
AND SUFFRAGIST SUSAN B. ANTHONY,
FROM 'EIGHTY YEARS AND MORE'

True love ennobles and dignifies the material labours of life; and homely services rendered for love's sake have in them a poetry that is immortal.

HARRIET BEECHER STOWE

One may be a very good friend and yet not of my opinion.

MARGARET CAVENDISH – FROM 'LETTERS'

Friendship of a kind that cannot easily be reversed tomorrow must have its roots in common interests and shared beliefs, and even between nations, in some personal feeling...

BARBARA TUCHMAN

A friend in need is a friend indeed.

PROVERB

When to the sessions of sweet silent thought
I summon up remembrance of things past,
I sigh the lack of many a thing I sought,
And with old woes new wail my dear time's waste:
Then can I drown an eye, unused to flow,
For precious friends hid in death's dateless night,
And weep afresh love's long-since-cancell'd woe,
And moan the expense of many a vanish'd sight;
Then can I grieve at grievances foregone,
And heavily from woe to woe tell o'er
The sad account of fore-bemoaned moan,
Which I new pay as if not paid before.
    But if the while I think on thee, dear friend,
    All losses are restored, and sorrows end.

WILLIAM SHAKESPEARE – 'SONNET 30'

'Give those girls a shout, Charles,' George said and helped himself to another drink.

But they were coming downstairs. They had left the room with its beds covered with clothes, its floor strewn with tissue-paper. They descended; the rose, the mauve, the white. Like a bunch of sweet-peas they looked, George thought.

'What a pretty frock, Frances,' Myra said, beginning with the worst. 'Poor pet,' she thought, and Frances guessed the thought, smiling primly and saying thank you.

'And such a lovely colour, Natalie,' Myra went on.

'But is it, though?' Natalie asked anxiously. 'And don't my shoes clash terribly? I think I look quite bleak in it, and it is last year's, really.'

Myra had scarcely wanted to go into all that. 'Now, Katie,' she began to say, as soon as she could. 'I don't think your friends know Benedict. And when you have introduced them we must be on our way. Your father and I have to go out to dinner after we've taken you to the dance. So who's to go with whom?'

ELIZABETH TAYLOR – FROM 'THE ROSE, THE MAUVE, THE WHITE'

We have fewer friends than we imagine, but more than we know.

HUGO VON HOFMANNSTHAL – FROM 'THE BOOK OF FRIENDS'

Your friend is your needs answered.
He is your field which you sow with love
   and reap with thanksgiving.
And he is your board and your fireside.
For you come to him with your hunger,
   and you seek him for peace.

KAHLIL GIBRAN

Have no friends not equal
   to yourself.

CONFUCIUS

Ah, yet, e'er I descend to th' grave
May I a small house, and large garden have!
And a few friends, and many books, both true,
Both wise, and both delightful too!

ABRAHAM COWLEY – FROM 'THE WISH'

Friendship is a serious affection; the most sublime of all affections, because it is founded on principle, and cemented by time. The very reverse may be said on love. In a great degree, love and friendship cannot subsist in the same bosom; even when inspired by different objects they weaken or destroy each other, and for the same object can only be felt in succession. The vain fears and fond jealousies, the winds which fan the flame of love, when judiciously or artfully tempered, are both incompatible with the tender confidence and sincere respect of friendship.

MARY WOLLSTONECRAFT

Where is Anne?
   Head above the buttercups,
Walking by the stream,
   Down among the buttercups.
Where is Anne?
   Walking with her man,
Lost in a dream,
   Lost among the buttercups.
What has she got in that little brown head?
Wonderful thoughts which can never be said.
What has she got in that firm little fist of hers?
Somebody's thumb, and it feels like Christopher's.
   Where is Anne?
   Close to her man.
   Brown head, gold head,
   In and out the buttercups.

A. A. MILNE – 'BUTTERCUP DAYS'

I am speaking now of the highest duty we owe our friends, the noblest, the most sacred – that of keeping their own nobleness, goodness, pure and incorrupt.... If we let our friend become cold and selfish and exacting without a remonstrance, we are no true lover, no true friend.

HARRIET BEECHER STOWE

Friendships, like geraniums, bloom in kitchens. Love runs up and down a flight of stairs and enters one flat and another...

BLANCHE H. GELFAUT

While lasting joys the man attend
Who has a faithful female friend.

CORNELIUS WHUR

Are we not like two volumes of one book?

MARCELINE DESBORDES-VALMORE – ON HER FRIENDSHIP
WITH PAULINE DUCHAMBGE

'Good night, young Copperfield,'
said Steerforth. 'I'll take care of you.'
    'You're very kind,' I gratefully returned.
'I am very much obliged to you.'
    'You haven't got a sister, have you?'
said Steerforth, yawning.
    'No,' I answered.
    'That's a pity,' said Steerforth. 'If you
had had one, I should think she would
have been a pretty, timid, little, bright-
eyed sort of girl. I should have liked to
know her. Good night, young
Copperfield.'
    'Good night, sir,' I replied.
    I thought of him very much after I went to
bed, and raised myself, I recollect, to look at
him where he lay in the moonlight, with his
handsome face turned up, and his head reclining easily on
his arm. He was a person of great power in my eyes...

CHARLES DICKENS – FROM 'DAVID COPPERFIELD'

Friendship is Love without his wings!

LORD GEORGE GORDON BYRON – FROM 'HOURS OF IDLENESS'

Friendship's an abstract of this noble flame,
'Tis love refin'd and purged from all its dross,
'Tis next to angel's love, if not the same,
As strong in passion is, though not so gross.

KATHERINE FOWLER PHILIPS – FROM 'FRIENDSHIP'

Others have their family; but to a solitary and an exile,
his friends are everything.

WILLA CATHER – FROM 'SHADOWS ON THE ROCK'

Love is like the wild rose-briar;
Friendship like the holly-tree.
The holly is dark when the rose-briar blooms,
But which will bloom most constantly?

EMILY BRONTË – FROM 'LOVE AND FRIENDSHIP'

Be more ready to visit a friend in
adversity than in prosperity.

GREEK PROVERB

Keep what is worth keeping
And with the breath of kindness
Blow the rest away.

DINAH MULOCK CRAIK – FROM 'FRIENDSHIP'

Little do men perceive, what solitude is, and how far it extendeth. For a crowd is not company; and faces are but a gallery of pictures; and talk but a tinkling cymbal, where there is no love. But we may go further, and affirm most truly: that it is a mere, and miserable solitude to want true friends; without which the world is but a wilderness.

The principal fruit of friendship is the ease and discharge of the fullness and swellings of the heart, which passions of all kinds do cause and induce. We know diseases of stoppings and suffocations are the most dangerous in the body; and it is not much otherwise in the mind. No receipt openeth the heart, but a true friend; to whom you may impart griefs, joys, fears, hopes, suspicions, counsels, and whatsoever lieth upon the heart, to oppress it, in a kind of civil shrift or confession.

The second fruit of friendship is healthful and sovereign for the understanding, as the first is for the affections. For friendship maketh indeed a fair day in the affections from storm and tempests: but it maketh daylight in the understanding, out of darkness and confusion of thoughts. . . . Add now, to make this second fruit of friendship complete, that other point, which lieth more open and falleth within vulgar observation; which is faithful counsel from a friend. There is as much difference between the counsel that a friend gives, and that a man giveth himself, as there is between the counsel of a friend and of a flatterer. For there is no such flatterer as is a man's self; and there is no such remedy against flattery of a man's self, as the liberty of a friend . . .

FRANCIS BACON

Yes'm, old friends is always best, 'less you can catch a new one that's fit to make an old one out of...

SARAH ORNE JEWETT

Two may talk together under the same roof for many years, yet never really meet, and two others at first speech are old friends.

MARY CATHERWOOD

A true friend is the most precious of all possessions and the one we take the least thought about acquiring.

LA ROCHEFOUCAULD

Officious, innocent, sincere, Of every friendless name the friend...

JAMES BOSWELL

'Tis hard to part when friends are dear,
Perhaps 'twill cost a sigh, a tear...

ANNA LAETITIA BARBAULD – FROM 'TO LIFE'

Best friend, my well-spring in the wilderness!

GEORGE ELIOT – FROM 'THE SPANISH GYPSY'

When Psyche's friend becomes her lover,
How sweetly these conditions blend!
But, oh, what anguish to discover
Her lover has become – her friend!

MADELINE BRIDGES – FROM 'FRIEND AND LOVER'

'Do you come to the play without knowing what it is?'

'Oh, yes, sir, yes, very frequently. I have no time to read play-bills. One merely comes to meet one's friends, and show that one's alive.'

FANNY BURNEY – FROM 'EVELINA'

Friendship is a disinterested commerce between equals; love, an abject intercourse between tyrants and slaves.

OLIVER GOLDSMITH – FROM 'THE GOOD NATUR'D MAN'

Life becomes either useless or insipid when we have no longer either friends or enemies.

QUEEN CHRISTINA OF SWEDEN

Though Love be deeper, Friendship is more wide...

CORINNE ROOSEVELT ROBINSON – FROM 'FRIENDSHIP'

'Tis midnight, and small thoughts have I of sleep;
Full seldom may my friend such vigils keep!
Visit him, gentle Sleep, with wings of healing,
And may this storm be but a mountain birth,
May all the stars hang bright above his dwelling,
Silent as tho' they *watch'd* the sleeping earth!
With light heart may he rise,
Gay fancy, cheerful eyes
And sing his lofty song and teach me to rejoice!

SAMUEL TAYLOR COLERIDGE – FROM 'DEJECTION, AN ODE'

Shortly Tom came upon the juvenile pariah of the village, Huckleberry Finn, son of the town drunkard. Huckleberry was cordially hated and dreaded by all the mothers of the town because he was idle, and lawless, and vulgar, and bad, and because all their children admired him so, and delighted in his forbidden society and wished they dared to be like him. Tom was like the rest of the respectable boys in that he envied Huckleberry his gaudy outcast condition, and was under strict orders not to play with him. So he played with him every time he got a chance.

MARK TWAIN – FROM
'THE ADVENTURES OF
TOM SAWYER'

'I don't want him,' said Rabbit. 'But it's always useful to know where a friend-and-relation is, whether you want him or whether you don't.'

A. A. MILNE – FROM 'THE HOUSE AT POOH CORNER'

It is a wonderful advantage to a man, in every pursuit of avocation, to secure an adviser in a sensible woman.... A man's best female friend is a wife of good sense and good heart who loves him.

EDWARD BULWER LYTTON

Be gentle to all and stern with yourself.

TERESA OF AVILA

When the sun shines on you, you
see your friends. Friends are the
thermometers by which one may judge
the temperature of one's fortunes.

MARGUERITE BLESSINGTON

O grant me, Heaven, a middle state,
Neither too humble nor too great;
More than enough, for nature's ends,
With something left to treat my friends.

DAVID MALLET — FROM 'IMITATION OF HORACE'

Talk not of love, it gives me pain,
For love hath been my foe;
He bound me with an iron chain,
And plunged me deep in woe.
But friendship's pure and lasting joys
My heart was formed to prove.

AGNES CRAIG – FROM 'TALK NOT OF LOVE'

Of all the heavenly gifts that mortal man commend,
What trusty treasure in the world can countervail a friend?

NICHOLAS GRIMALD

Treat your friends as you do your pictures, place them in the best light.

LADY SPENCER CHURCHILL

To like and dislike the same things,
that is indeed true friendship.

SALLUST – FROM 'CATILINE'

And we find at the end of a perfect day,
The soul of a friend we've made.

CARRIE JACOBS BOND – FROM 'A PERFECT DAY'

There are two elements that go to the composition of friendship, each so sovereign that I can detect no superiority in either, no reason why either should be first named. One is truth. A friend is a person with whom I may be sincere. Before him I may think aloud. I am arrived at last in the presence of a man so real and equal, that I may drop even those undermost garments of dissimulation, courtesy and second thought which men never put off, and may deal with him with the simplicity and wholeness with which one chemical atom meets another. Sincerity is the luxury allowed, like diadems and authority, only to the highest rank, that being permitted to speak the truth.... The other element of friendship is tenderness. We are holden to men by every sort of tie, by blood, by pride, by fear, by hope, by lucre, by lust, by hate, by administration, by every circumstance, and badge, and trifle, but we can scarcely believe that so much character can subsist in another as to draw us by love. Can another be so blessed, and we so pure, that we can offer him tenderness? When a man becomes dear to me, I have touched the goal of fortune.

RALPH WALDO EMERSON –
'FRIENDSHIP'

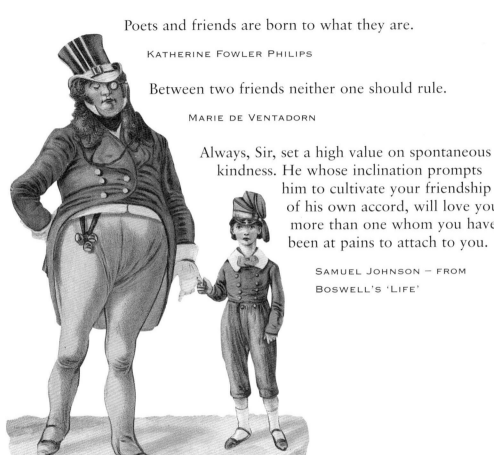

Poets and friends are born to what they are.

KATHERINE FOWLER PHILIPS

Between two friends neither one should rule.

MARIE DE VENTADORN

Always, Sir, set a high value on spontaneous
kindness. He whose inclination prompts
him to cultivate your friendship
of his own accord, will love you
more than one whom you have
been at pains to attach to you.

SAMUEL JOHNSON — FROM
BOSWELL'S 'LIFE'

If I can stop one heart from breaking
I shall not live in vain;
If I can ease one life the aching,
Or cool one pain
Or help one fainting robin
Unto his nest again,
I shall not live in vain.

EMILY DICKINSON

Looks are its food, its nectar sighs,
Its couch the lips, its throne the eyes,
The soul its breath: and so possest,
Heaven't raptures reign in mortal breast.

MARIA BROOKS — FROM 'FRIENDSHIP'

A friend should bear his friend's infirmities...

SHAKESPEARE – 'JULIUS CAESAR' IV III 85

Gentle ladies, you will remember till old age
What we did together in our brilliant youth.

SAPPHO

When he was asked 'What is
a friend?' he said 'One soul
inhabiting two bodies.'

DIOGENES LAERTIUS,
REFERRING TO THE
PHILOSOPHER
ARISTOTLE

You may be sure that she showed Rebecca over every room of the house, and everything in every one of her drawers; and her books, and her piano, and her dresses, and all her necklaces, brooches, laces, and gimcracks. She insisted upon Rebecca accepting the white cornelian and the turquoise rings, and a sweet sprigged muslin, which was too small for her now, though it would fit her friend to a nicety; and she determined in her heart to ask her mother's permission to present her white Cashmere shawl to her friend. Could she not spare it? – and had not her brother Joseph just brought her two from India?

When Rebecca saw the two magnificent Cashmere shawls which Joseph Sedley had brought home to his sister, she said, with perfect truth, 'that it must be delightful to have a brother,' and easily got the pity of the tender-hearted Amelia, for being alone in the world, an orphan without friends of kindred.

'Not alone,' said Amelia; 'you know, Rebecca, I shall always be your friend – indeed I will.'

W. M. THACKERAY – FROM 'VANITY FAIR'

There's a kind of emotional exploration
you plumb with a friend that you
don't really do with your family.

BETTE MIDLER

To act the part of a true friend
requires more conscientious
feeling than to fill with credit
and complacency any other
station or capacity in social life.

SARAH ELLIS

...that free communication of
letters and opinions, just as they
arise... which is the only
groundwork of friendship.

MARY ANN LAMB — ON HER FRIENDSHIP
WITH HER BROTHER, CHARLES

I have often thought, that as longevity is generally desired, and, I believe, generally expected, it would be wise to be continually adding to the number of our friends, that the loss of some may be supplied by others. Friendship, 'the wine of life', should, like a well-stocked cellar, be thus continually renewed; and it is consolatory to think, that although we can seldom add what will equal the generous first-growths of our youth, yet friendship becomes insensibly old in much less time than is commonly imagined, and not many years are required to make it very mellow and pleasant. Warmth will, no doubt, make a considerable difference. Men of affectionate temper and bright fancy will coalesce a great deal sooner than those who are cold and dull.

Johnson said to Sir Joshua Reynolds, 'If a man does not make new acquaintance as he advances through life, he will soon find himself left alone. A man, Sir, should keep his friendship in constant repair.'

JAMES BOSWELL

A faythfulle frende wold I fayne fynde,
To fynde hym where he myghte be founde.
But now is the world wext so unkynde,
Yet frendship is fall to the grounde;
Now a frende I have founde...

JULIANA BERNERS

...that perfect tranquillity of life,
which is nowhere to be found but
in retreat, a faithful friend and a
good library.

APHRA BEHN — FROM
'THE LUCKY MISTAKE'

Friend of my bosom, thou more than a brother,
Why were thou not born in my father's dwelling?
So might we talk of the old familiar faces...

CHARLES LAMB — FROM
'THE OLD FAMILIAR FACES'

There can be no friendship where there is no freedom. Friendship loves a free air, and will not be penned up in straight and narrow enclosures. It will speak freely, and act so, too; and take nothing ill where no ill is meant; nay, where it is, 'twill easily forgive, and forget too, upon small acknowledgements.

Friends are true twins in soul; they sympathise in everything.

One is not happy without the other, nor can either of them be miserable alone, as if they could change bodies, they take their turns in pain as well as in pleasure; relieving one another in their most adverse conditions.

What one enjoys, the other cannot want. Like the primitive Christians, they have all things in common, and no property but in one another.

A true friend unbosoms freely, advises justly, assists readily, adventures boldly, takes all patiently, defends courageously, and continues a friend unchangeably.

The covetous, the angry, the proud, the jealous, the talkative, cannot but make ill friends, as well as the false. In short, choose a friend as thou dost a wife, till death separate you.

WILLIAM PENN

A friend must not be wounded, even in jest.

LATIN PROVERB

Our goal should be to achieve joy.

ANA CASTILLO – FROM 'MASSACRE OF THE DREAMERS'

But every road is tough to me
That has no friend to cheer it ...

ELIZABETH SHANE

Friendship, like heraldry, is hereby known
Richest when plainest, bravest when alone ...

KATHERINE PHILIPS

In early days, and calmer hours,
When heart with heart delights to blend,
Where bloom my native valley's bowers –
I had – Ah! have I now? – a friend! –
To him this pledge I charge thee send –
Memorial of a youthful vow...

LORD GEORGE GORDON BYRON – FROM 'THE GIAOUR'

Think where man's glory most begins and ends
And say my glory was I had such friends.

W. B. YEATS – FROM 'THE MUNICIPAL GALLERY REVISITED'

Should auld acquaintance be forgot
And never brought to min'?
Should auld acquaintance be forgot
And auld lang syne?

For auld lang syne, my dear,
For auld lang syne,
We'll tak a cup o' kindness yet,
For auld lang syne.

We twa hae paidled i' the burn,
From morning sun till dine;
But seas between us braid hae roar'd
Sin' auld lang syne...

ROBERT BURNS – FROM 'AULD LANG SYNE'

The possibility of Mr Collins's fancying himself in love with her friend had once occurred to Elizabeth within the last day or two; but that Charlotte could encourage him, seemed almost as far from possibility as that she could encourage him herself, and her astonishment was consequently so great as to overcome at first the bounds of decorum, and she could not help crying out,

'Engaged to Mr Collins! my dear Charlotte, – impossible!'

The steady countenance which Miss Lucas had commanded in telling her story, gave way to a momentary confusion here on receiving so direct a reproach; though, as it was no more than she expected, she soon regained her composure, and calmly replied,

'Why should you be surprised, my dear Eliza? – Do you think it incredible that Mr Collins should be able to procure any woman's good opinion, because he was not so happy as to succeed with you?'

But Elizabeth had now recollected herself, and making a strong effort for it, was able to assure her with tolerable firmness that the prospect of their relationship was highly grateful to her, and that she wished her all imaginable happiness...

JANE AUSTEN – FROM 'PRIDE AND PREJUDICE'

The balm of life, a kind and faithful friend.

MERCY OTIS WARREN

Friends should consider themselves as the sacred guardians of each other's virtue; and the noblest testimony they can give of their affections is the correction of the faults of those they love.... Happy is he to whom, in the maturer season of life, there remains one tried and constant friend.

ANNA LAETITIA BARBAULD – FROM 'ON FRIENDSHIP'

I have always detested the belief that sex is the chief bond between man and woman. Friendship is far more human.

AGNES SMEDLEY

Be courteous to all, but intimate with few, and let those few be well tried before you give them your confidence. True friendship is a plant of slow growth, and must undergo and withstand the shocks of adversity before it is entitled to the appellation.

GEORGE WASHINGTON – LETTER

With rue my heart is laden
For golden friends I had
For many a rose-lipt maiden
And many a lightfoot lad.

A. E. HOUSMAN – FROM 'A SHROPSHIRE LAD'

Friendship is a noble name, 'tis love refined.

SUSANNAH CENTLIVRE

Lord, make me coy and tender to offend:
In friendship, first I think, if that agree
Which I intend,
Unto my friend's intent and end.
I would not use a friend as I use Thee.

GEORGE HERBERT – FROM 'UNKINDNESS'

A thing of beauty is a joy for ever:
Its loveliness increases; it will never
Pass into nothingness; but still will keep
A bower quiet for us, and a sleep
Full of sweet dreams, and health, and quiet breathing.
Therefore, on every morrow, are we wreathing
A flowery band to bind us to the earth,
Spirit of despondence, of the inhuman dearth
Of noble natures, of the gloomy days,
Of all the unhealthy and o'er-darkened ways
Made for our searching; yes, in spite of all,
Some shape of beauty moves away the pall
From our dark spirits...

JOHN KEATS – FROM 'ENDYMION'

The happiest people seem to be those who have no particular reason for being happy except they are so.

W. R. INGE

Happiness is a how, not a what; a talent, not an object.

HERMANN HESSE – 'LETTERS'

One cannot divine
nor forecast the conditions
that will make happiness; one
only stumbles upon them by
chance, in a lucky hour, at the world's
end somewhere, and holds fast to the days,
as to fortune or fame.

WILLA CATHER – FROM 'WILLA CATHER IN EUROPE'

I might give my life for my friend, but he had better not ask me to do up a parcel.

Logan Pearsall Smith

To my friends, pictured within.

Sir Edward Elgar – Dedication to the 'Enigma Variations'

Love is blind, friendship closes its eyes.

Proverb

Green be the turf above thee,
Friend of my better days!
None knew thee but to love thee,
Nor named thee but to praise.

Fitz-Greene Halleck – from 'On the Death of Joseph Rodman Drake'